Discover Thanksgiving

by Juliana O'Neill

© 2018 by Juliana O'Neill
ISBN: 978-1-5324-0828-1
eISBN: 978-1-5324-0827-4
Images licensed from Fotolia.com and Adobe Stock
All rights reserved.
No portion of this book may be reproduced without
express permission of the publisher.
First Edition
Published in the United States by
Xist Publishing
www.xistpublishing.com
PO Box 61593 Irvine, CA 92602

Thanksgiving is a national holiday in the United States of America. Thanksgiving is always celebrated on the fourth Thursday in November.

On Thanksgiving, people gather around a table to eat a big meal. Friends and family give thanks for the past year.

Thanksgiving began as a celebration of the Pilgrim's first harvest.

Native Americans helped English colonists grow food. Once the food was ready to eat, it was time to celebrate.

Kids sometimes perform plays about the first Thanksgiving.

They also make crafts to celebrate the friendship between the settlers and the Native Americans.

Families decorate their homes and yards for Thanksgiving.

Today, the Thanksgiving holiday is still centered around a feast. Different families have different traditions.

Turkey is the most traditional main dish.

People also make lots of side dishes like mashed potatoes, stuffing, cranberry sauce, and green beans.

Families from different parts of the United States often make different foods. These regional foods spread as people move and build families with people from other places.

Thanksgiving weekend is one of the biggest travel times of the year. Families fill airports and roads to be together and share a meal.

On Thanksgiving, people play games like football. People also watch football on TV.

Thanksgiving is a holiday for family members to work and play together.

Thanksgiving dinner is not complete without a slice of pumpkin pie. It is an all-American dessert for an all-American holiday.